CW00428124

For Sarah, Thomas, Lucy & Joel

BEYOND THE ANGEL

Developed by Damien Wootten
Designed by Andrew Houghton
Scans by Jack Lowe
Published by photoNORTH
Distributed by Zymurgy Publishing

ISBN: 0-9546001-2-6

BEYOND THE ANGEL

DAMIEN WOOTTEN

photoNORTH

PREFACE

During the Depression, Roy Stryker, director of the FSA, commissioned American photographers Russell Lee, Dorothea Lange and Walker Evans "to show city people what it's like to live on the farm". Not only were they to focus on rural communities and agricultural workers, they were to show these people at a crucially significant time, undergoing extreme economic hardship.

This was to be a seminal moment in the development of documentary photography. This was photography with a purpose - a specific and highly charged photography enlisted to tell stories, circulated around the world through magazines such as 'Life' and 'Look'.

The last five years have seen a quieter, but no less significant upheaval and transformation here in this country to the lives of people who make a living from farming and agricultural work. The 2003 Agricultural Review reported that in 2002 almost eighteen thousand farmers and farm workers lost their jobs. In the six years up to 2002 over sixty five thousand people left the industry. Government figures show the average UK income for a farmer in 2002/3 was a mere £11,100.

Damien Wootten's black and white photographs have a clear purpose and are part of that same tradition of photographers who feel they have something to say. This project emerges from a friendship with Ann and Hugh Gray and their two young children. The family run Ravensworth Grange, a farm on the southern edge of Gateshead, part of the rural/urban fringe and just within

sight of the Angel of the North. Returning over a number of years, he has photographed change here, gaining an intimacy and insight into the life and work of one family.

There is an urgency here, and a will to communicate the pressures and the constant struggle of running a farm. Damien's open style, his use of wide angle and grainy fast film means we are plunged from light into dark, from bleak mid-winter to high summer. Work and leisure activities are central to the cycle of contrasts that make up this narrative and though it is just one family, it appears to be representative of something collective.

John Grundy's essay creates a vivid portrait of this farm, its setting in the landscape, as well as its historical place. His essay skilfully traces a continuous thread of change in the land, conveying the sense of responsibility that we must take in developing a deeper understanding of modern farming and food production in the twenty-first century.

Alessandro Vincentelli

Curator at BALTIC,
Centre for Contemporary Art in Gateshead

RAVENSWORTH GRANGE FARM

The kitchen of Hugh and Ann Gray's farmhouse at Ravensworth Grange near Kibblesworth on the southern edge of Gateshead is pretty much what you would expect a farmhouse kitchen to be. There's a big old cream coloured Aga or Raeburn type stove in an alcove at one side and a low-beamed ceiling. Down the middle of the room is a long scrubbed deal table and the walls are obscured by assorted old dressers and things. There are wellies and boots and well-worn Barbour coats all over the place and the sort of detritus you might expect in the kitchen of a working farm. It's not exactly cosy much of the time because they're tough, the Grays, and don't feel the need to shut the door, but it is a very attractive, lived-in, and traditional farmhouse kitchen. The picture changes, however, if you walk out of the back door - you are confronted by a vision of England which is not at all traditional and manages to be at exactly the same time incredibly distinctive and yet ever so typical of the country as a whole.

You are in the countryside and there are fields all around you. To your left is a stone walled garden with beautiful gnarled old cherry trees. The farm track climbs across a bare hillside, the edges of the view framed by stands of old trees. There are assorted cows and sheep, and pigs in bijou little Anderson shelters. It's an attractive but unremarkable rural view - nice but only just pretty.

But if you look to the right from the back door the view is anything but unremarkable. It is in fact extraordinary. When these photographs of Damien's were taken, it was a view partly obliterated by the vast scar of an open-cast coal mine which had replaced all of the lower fields on the farm and by the bleak earthen bank that separated the mine workings from the house and farmyard. At that time the juxtaposition was astonishing - rural

England jammed savagely, cheek by jowl, against industrial England. Well, the open-cast mine has gone now, its allotted time has ended and the hillside has been sensitively restored back into fields again, but in some ways the view remains as odd as it did before.

There's a lot of sky, first of all, beautiful sky. The farm is high up on a hillside and the view to the north and east is pretty immense. The first time I was there was latish on a winter's afternoon and the evening sun poured over the shoulder of the hill behind the farm and lit up the landscape to the east in glorious relief. It made the scene seem very beautiful - but it is, I have to say, a very odd sort of loveliness.

Now that the open-cast mine has gone, the foreground is just what you might expect a farming landscape to be like - rural England, quite beautiful and green, rolling and varied, banks of trees and little knots of buildings, stone-built farms and cottages dotted among the fields. In the background though, beyond this traditional farming landscape, are the towns of Gateshead and Washington - a vast urban sprawl of motorways and towerblocks, terraces and housing estates - mile after mile of town spread along the side of the valley and glimpsed on other hillsides out towards the east and the distant sea. In the valley bottom, in the middle distance, lies the industrial park of the Team Valley with its ordered 1930s rows of model factories and its lurid 1990s ranges of factory outlet stores and cheap warehouse shops, and in the centre of the whole view, the bull's eye as it were, is Antony Gormley's giant sculpture, The Angel of the North, towering motionless and toughly serene over the constant stream of traffic on the motorway below.

It's an amazing view, one of those love-it-or-hate-it views. Most people do love the beauty of a pure English landscape; almost as many, I imagine, are excited by the intense energy of towns and cities. But this is neither one thing nor the other, it's not completely rural but it's not truly urban either. It fascinates me, though, because it's the world that most of us actually live in. We live on the edges of towns and on the edges of countryside and the juxtaposition of the two is the landscape we know best but look at least. Although they're not often as dramatic, not often as hilly as the view from Ravensworth Grange, every town has views on its ragged edges which are more or less like this one.

If you look carefully, though, there are plenty of clues that this is not anywhere, that it's the North East of England you're looking at. The landscape is bare and undemonstrative. Trees are few and far between. The older houses are all built of

blackened sandstone and everywhere there are reminders of the area's industrial past. Antony Gormley's Gateshead Angel, built in distressed steel, with its angel's wings as rigid and mechanical as a bridge or a plane, is a brilliant contemporary personification of the tough no-nonsense industrial history of this place. In the valley bottom there are the vestiges of the Kibblesworth pit and the brick works that accompanied it. Down the side of the farm and up the valley side opposite, is the line of the Bowes Railway, one of the early railways that carried coal from the mines of inland Durham to the coal staithes on the Tyne at Jarrow. On the hillsides towards inner Gateshead are the terraces of workers' cottages and the rows of Tyneside flats.

So here we are, standing at the back door of Hugh and Ann's farmhouse, at the intersection of two worlds; a working farm right on the very edge of the farming world, right on the edge of the town, in the crack between the paving stones as it were. It doesn't feel like an easy place to make a living

But they've been at it for a long time. Hugh Gray was born here forty-something years ago and the family has been farming in the area for much longer than that. The site of the farm where Hugh's great-grandfather lived in the 1880s is visible from the back door of the present farmhouse but its buildings have been turned into housing and its fields long ago sold to other farms. The family has been at Ravensworth Grange since 1888 - so they've had to live with their towny and industrial neighbours for many years. They've watched the pits close and the opencast mine come and go. They've watched the farms disappear beneath factories and the factories turn into shops. From their position high up on the hill they've watched the housing estates being built and the roads grow. They've watched the endless increase in the number of cars. They've watched the town swell out towards them in waves. Even the farms around them have changed, many of the farmhouses converted into elegant middle-class country houses, the land bought up by a few expanding farms. And in the middle of all of this extraordinary hotch-potch of contemporary Britain is Ravensworth Grange, 200 acres of mixed owner-occupied farming on the edge of all this change. It doesn't, as I said, seem a very easy thing to do.

I read the papers and watch TV and it is obvious to me, like it is to everybody else, that farming in Britain is going through hard times. It's not just the high profile horrors like BSE and Foot and Mouth that cause the problems but the constant drip feed of pressures - pressures from cheaper producers abroad, from supermarkets forcing down prices to farmers, from consumers demanding a more and more perfect and impossibly homogenous product. There are clearly other pressures too, social pressures - to escape from the risk and isolation of the countryside into easier and safer occupations elsewhere. I used to be a Listed Building Fieldworker working for English Heritage and I remember one farmer in north Northumberland telling me that in his youth, his farm - a huge farm in a glorious situation on the coast - had been home and workplace to more than fifty people - to farmworkers, milkmaids, children. The buildings had been constantly active, the farm cottages filled with families. But now, he told me, he worked it alone, cocooned even from the wind off the sea by the cab of his mighty John Deere.

As a Listed Building man I was constantly confronted on farms by another more practical problem, an architectural problem. I found farmers bemoaning their ancient farm buildings, wondering what on earth they could do to make them useful in the modern world and how they could afford the big modern sheds which would accept modern machinery and suit the styles of contemporary farming.

At first glance the farm buildings on Hugh and Ann's farm seem like an ideal illustration of this problem. They suggest that times have been as hard here as anywhere else. The Ravensworth buildings that were ideal and well organised for 19th century farming are untidy now, even tumbledown in places. There is mud and bits of machinery dotted around the entrances; walls and roofs have holes in them. They aren't picturesque. Tourist brochures wouldn't choose them to market the area. You could be excused for thinking they'd been abandoned. Inside the smells are intense, unsettling to a visitor from the town and the noises are even more unsettling - a constant low undertone of grunts and snuffles because these pens contain pigs, extraordinary pigs.

I was a little bit frightened of them if the truth be told. I've always been frightened of pigs and these are a touch more unnerving than most, especially the boar who has something of a nightmare quality about him. He's big, well actually he's gigantic with tusks and bad breath and when he gets his feet up on the walls of his pen and peers over he could scare for England.

I'm not big on pigs, it would be generous to describe my knowledge of them as limited, but I have been told that these Middle Whites are a traditional breed and their presence

in these buildings (and, to be fair, in the Anderson shelters too) is one of the keys to this whole story.

Locally-reared meat from traditional breeds of animals has become Hugh and Ann's chosen route out of the doldrums of modern British farming. Others have chosen different ways. Some struggle on. Many have sold off their buildings to housing developers or converted the farmworkers' cottages into holiday lets. Some have opened up their premises to other industries - small-scale contemporary industries or more traditional rural ones, or both. Some have killed themselves or sold up entirely and moved on to a different way of life. I know of a few farmers who turned themselves into model organic farms and invite visitors to farm walks. Some have cafes or make jam; lots take in visitors for bed and breakfast. Most do one or more of these things while still slogging away at the day job of working the land. It's a source of continuous astonishment to me how a group of people like farmers, not normally considered to be adventurous free-thinkers, should have shown so much initiative and energy into finding ways to alleviate their collective crisis.

Hugh and Ann's way, as I said, is to produce quality meat and sell it at special farmers' markets around the region. To help them do this, they have already converted one range of their outmoded farm buildings into a spanking new meat cutting room and cold store. It is white and steel, echoing and antiseptic, the antithesis it seems of everything else on the farm. Isn't that odd? Isn't it odd that the whitest, gleamiest, most modern place on the farm should be where the battle for traditional values is taking place? Isn't it odd, too, the worlds that farmers inhabit - stepping a few paces from a world that farmers have known for thousands of years - into the bright, industrial efficiency of the 21st century?

I feel as if I've written about the Grays' farm as if it's a metaphor for modern Britain and modern farming, and in a way you could say that it is. Its problems and solutions are certainly representative of the country as a whole and shared by lots of other farmers; but nobody wants to be just a metaphor and Ravensworth certainly isn't. As Damien's photographs show, this farm is a real place with real people. It's a unique place too. In some ways characteristic of modern Britain - but there's nowhere else quite like it.

John Grundy

"The barn was very large. It was very old. It smelled of hay and it smelled of manure...and the wonderful sweet breath of patient cows. It often had a sort of peaceful smell - as though nothing bad could happen ever again in the world"

Charlotte's Web - E.B. White

RAVENSWORTH GRANGE FARM

2000 - 2003

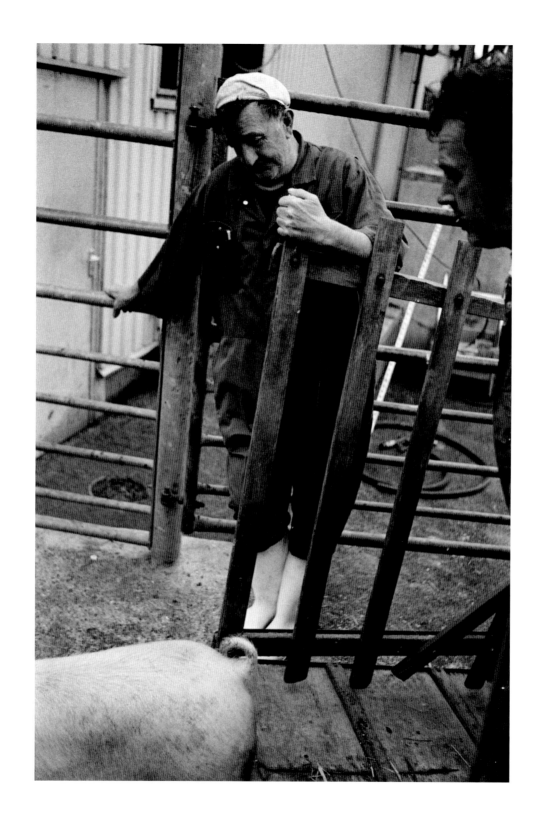

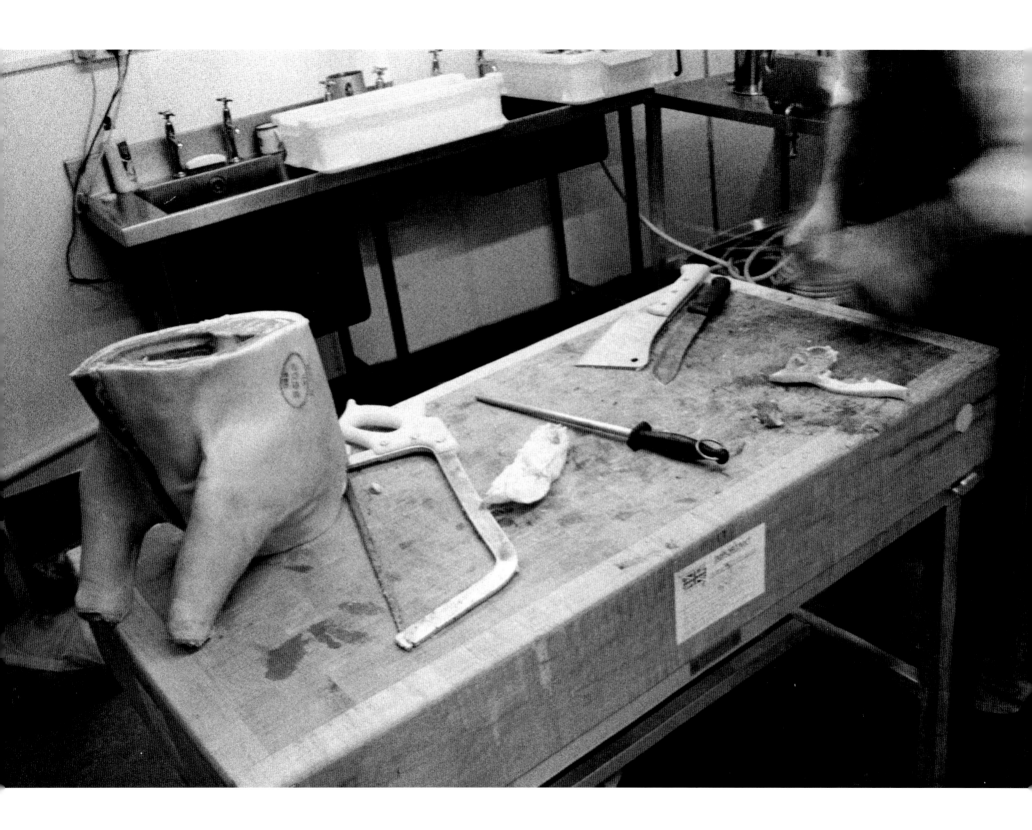

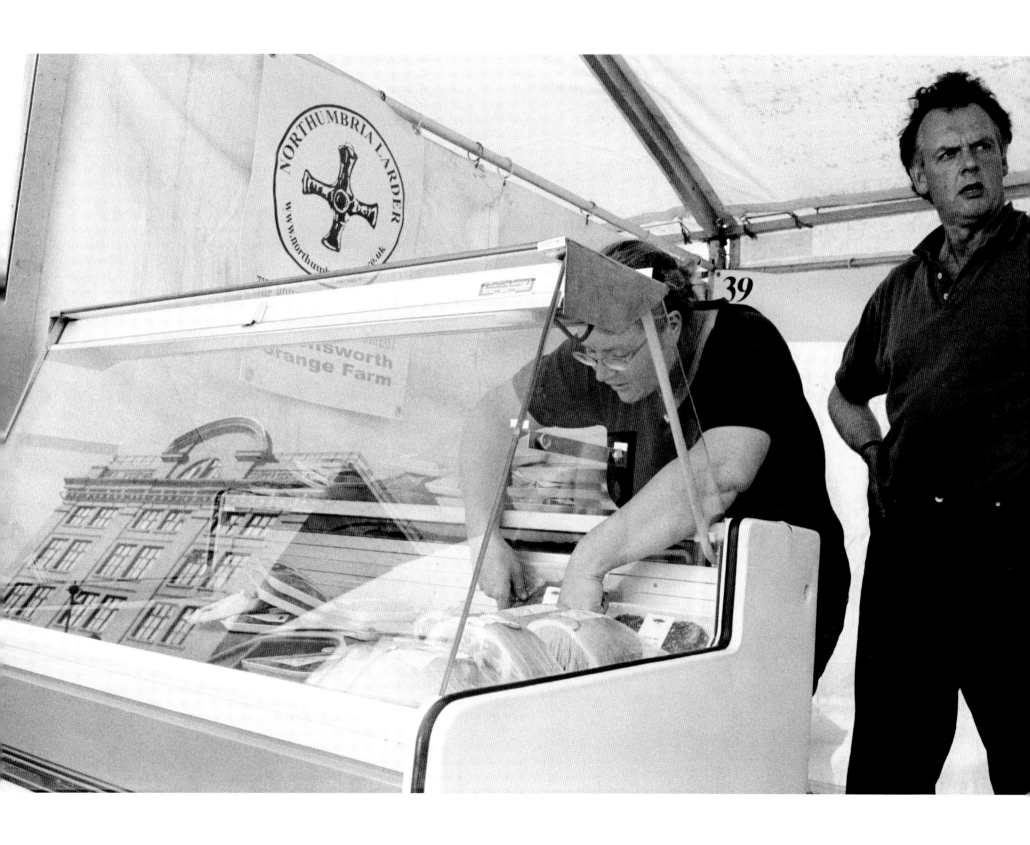

Beyond the Angel is published to coincide with a touring exhibition and has been made possible with the support of the following:

Arts Council England
Gateshead Council
Tynemouth College
photoNORTH
Foundry Media

Exhibition dates:

The Gallery, Gateshead Library
8th January to 19th February 2005

Arts Centre Washington
25th February to 9th April 2005

Lamplight Arts Centre, Stanley
18th April to 20th May 2005

I would like to thank Hugh and Ann Gray, Vicki Gray, John Grundy, Martin Ellis, Andy Houghton, Alessandro Vincentelli, Jack Lowe, Thomas Wootten, Lynn Knight, June O Malley, Pauline Haughey, Martin Weston, Jane Hewison, Jim Ward, Jon Houghton and Andrew Rothwell. Thanks also to my friends and family, particularly my wife Sarah and my parents, Steve and Mary Wootten, for their help, advice and interest throughout the development of the project.

Damien Wootten.

photoNORTH is an initiative supporting photography and photographers in the North-East.
For further information visit www.photo-north.net